ISBN-13: 9798699225835
ISBN-10: 1477123456

Cover design by: Art Painter
Library of Congress Control Number: 2018675309
Printed in the United States of America

RAY'S VICTORY

*One little brown dog's journey from
fighter to family member*

Jacqueline C Johnson

This book is dedicated to the men and women in Animal Welfare who put their hearts on the line every single day for dogs like Ray. But this book is especially for the people Ray had the good fortune to know and love.
My husband Kevin Johnson
Justyne Moore
Doctor Patti Patterson
Doctor Chris Hanson
Tom Williams
Kathy Moore
McKenzie Garcia
Patti Lindh
Michelle Logan
John Garcia
Mileen Keating
Carissa Hendrick
Jen Sevrud
Tamara Dormer
Cherie Mascis
And a special thank you to all of Ray's friends and fans who willingly provided many of the pictures in this book and permission to use them.

I do need to recognize two special photographers.
Kerry Johnson Bowers took all the shots used at the SD anti-bsl rally. She captured Ray's personality perfectly.
Justyne Moore is a incredible individual who has played a special part in my life and the lives of all my dogs. I could have made a book out of the photos Justyne has taken. I have often laughed and said she was our personal photographer.

CONTENTS

INTRODUCTION

When I started this project Ray was still with us. I could tell he was starting to fail, and I wanted something tangible to celebrate his life. Now that he is gone, this tribute becomes even more important.

I decided to leave the "Forward by Ray" in this book. This is primarily a joyous look at a dog's ability to overcome and forgive, and I think his voice is an important part of that work. And even though Ray has left the physical world, he still manifests himself around me. In honor of all the things he taught me, I need to leave his words in place.

People may be disappointed by the quality of some of the photos in this book. But I didn't have a professional photographer following us around every day. In order to give you a real taste of his life, I have to use the photos that were available. Many of them were taken by friends and family who met and fell in love with Ray. I sincerely thank them for giving me permission to include them in this book.

There is no way to adequate explain the effect Ray had

on people. He was so calm and dignified at the end of his life. He radiated love and acceptance for every person who took the time to meet him. He patiently posed with hundreds of people who wanted a picture with him. He seemed to understand that he stood for something much, much bigger than himself. He would sit in the sun and soak up the admiration. In fact, if for some reason we didn't go down to lunch, he would spend the rest of the day trying to pull me towards the Village. It was definitely his happy place.

The Vicktory Dogs showed an entire nation that dogs did not need to be defined by the abuse they had suffered. That even though they had endured horrible experiences, they were ready and willing to trust humans. That is a very humbling thing.

I hope you enjoy this glimpse into Ray's life. I know that I will never be the same after our time together. If I am honest with myself, I have to admit that Ray picked his time to leave us. He had fulfilled his purpose, and he moved on. I think he knew that I would do everything I could to keep him with me, and he saved me from having to make that final, heart-breaking decision.

HE WAS SUCH A UNIQUE LITTLE DOG..........

Painting by Levity Thomkinson. One of her Re51liant 51 Project.

FORWARD

by Ray the Vicktory Dog

My name is Ray, but you "probably know me as Ray the Vicktory Dog. My mom says I'm just a naughty little brown dog who she adores! The first thing I want to say is that in many ways I am just like any other dog…although in some ways my story, and that of the other Vicktory Dogs, is truly unique.

In April of 2007, police executed a search warrant on the home of football player Michael Vick in Surrey County, Virginia. They did not expect to find a full dog fighting operation, including more than 50 pit bulls, training equipment and paraphernalia unique to dog fighting.

I was one of those dogs. At the time of our seizure it was a common belief that fighting dogs were beyond redemption and must be euthanized. This time concerned groups and individuals went to the court and convinced the judge to have each dog assessed individually.

It surprised everyone involved when all but one of the dogs passed their evaluation. Many of the dogs went directly into foster care or rescue. The 22 most challenging dogs, including me, went to Best Friends Animal Society's Sanctuary in Kanab, Utah.

When we arrived at the sanctuary on January 2, 2009, trainers, caregivers and behavioral specialists were on hand to begin assessing and working with us immediately. When one of the caregivers, Mileen, opened my crate, I was so cold, tired and frightened that I crawled up under her coat and nestled under her chin. I am so human-oriented that I turned to a person I didn't even know for comfort.

It didn't take long for me to get the reputation of being an overly-excitable goof. I would get so happy when my caregivers would come to see me that I would jump up and grab their clothes, or snatch the leash and run away with it. Many different people worked with me, trying to help me learn the skills I needed in order to be adopted. But it was very hard for me to learn, because I was just so very excited.

My parents, who worked at the sanctuary in the parrot department, decided to take me on as a project dog. They had worked together with other Vicktory Dogs, and were able to help them pass their court-ordered Canine Good Citizen (CGC) tests, so they could be adopted.

Mom and Dad make an awesome team. Mom's job was to work with the trainers to teach me the skills I needed to know to pass my CGC. Dad's job was to be the fun person. Every day he would walk and play with me without any pressure. We walked for miles; sometimes just the two of us and sometimes with another caregiver and dog to help me become less fearful. I have had some bad experiences with other dogs, and they can scare me.

Six years after I was rescued, on August 13, 2013, I passed my CGC, and was ready to be adopted. My parents had to pass a court-ordered Federal background check and meet other requirements before they could take me home. I had to be a foster dog with them for six months before my adoption was final on Valentine's Day, 2014. I was finally home. Now I live with a very old cat, 7 parrots and another rescued fighting dog, McCaela the Turtle. My house is noisy and chaotic...but that's ok, because it's home.

This book is a photo chronical of my life since the day I met my parents.

BACKGROUND

I can remember watching the news when the Vick bust happened in 2007. How horrifying the stories were as they came out. I watched the news clips of dogs being removed from the property at the end of catch poles. And I believed, as much of the rest of the country did, that these dogs were too vicious and damaged to ever be considered safe. How wrong we all were.

That same year I started watching an amazing show on the National Geographic Channel....DogTown. My husband and I religiously watched it every week for the next 4 seasons. The episode that touched me the most was the one about the 22 Vicktory Dogs who were sent to Best Friends Animal Society for rehabilitation (or as
Little Red's mom says "recovery").

I needed to know more about this amazing place called Best Friends. So I began checking in on their website every couple of days, reading all the stories, rejoicing and grieving with the successes and losses. It wasn't long before I started checking out the job page as well.

In November of 2009 I made a pilgrimage to the sanctuary in Kanab, Utah. What I saw there convinced me that this is where Kevin and I were meant to be. The canyon itself is breathtakingly beautiful: Thousands of acres of red rock and sand in the middle of nowhere. It is almost a kingdom unto itself. The staff is made up of like-minded people who share a common mission: ending the killing of healthy dogs and cats in America's shelters. This magical place is home to 1700 animals on any given day, each loved and cared for until their permanent family arrives. During my tour of the facility, the tour guide pointed out a very special sight, Little Red, the Vicktory Dog being walked by her caregiver. I felt as if I'd just seen a celebrity.

After my visit to Best Friends I found it very hard to settle back in to my regular life. Kevin and I decided that it didn't make financial sense to give up our jobs to move across the country for less than half the pay. That is what our heads kept telling us.....but my heart had already decided that it had found the right place for me to live.

Six month later I was called by the current manager of the Parrot Department and offered the chance of a lifetime; to become the new department manager. An incredible opportunity to work at my heart's passion, helping to bring about a time when there are no more animals killed simply because they didn't have a home.

SQUEAKER AND OSCAR

Most of the offices here at the sanctuary have dogs (or cats) who come spend the day, returning to their runs at night. It gives them a break from the high energy of Dog-Town, allows them some extra socialization, and starts to help them become familiar wth indoor settings. Offices allow dogs to experience many things they will encounter in a home; ringing phones, visitors and constant interruptions.

In 2011 I asked the DogTown managers if I could have an office dog at Parrots. I wasn't too concerned about which dog it was, just that he or she didn't have a high prey drive, which could put our birds in jeopardy.

Michelle Logan, DogTown co-manager, suggested Vicktory Dogs Squeaker and Oscar. So for one day a week, these two shy kids came to spend the day with us. I loved having dogs in my office. It was great to have an excuse to stop and take a walk. They kept me company throughout the day. And, after settling in, they seemed to enjoy the novelty of life in the Parrot Building.

It was such a good fit that I decided one day a week just wasn't enough! When I asked if they could spend more time with us, Michelle surprised me by suggesting they move in to Parrots. Both Squeaker and Oscar were obviously benefitting from their time away from DogTown, and there were dogs waiting to come to the sanctuary. By moving them to my office permanently, it would free up space for others. So, we installed a dog run and a doggie door in my office, and we moved the kids over to Parrots.

Squeaker wasn't with us very long. Shortly after moving over she needed to have ACL surgery on her cruciate ligament. A successful surgery requires a long recuperation, so Squeak moved over to the clinic for rehab after surgery.

In addition, she already had bonded with the person who would eventually adopt her. Squeaker's mom, who is a tech at the clinic, had worked with her every single day for more than a year, helping her recover enough to pass her Canine Good Citizen test. Once she passed the test, Squeaker went home to begin her 6 month, court-ordered foster period.

Oscar was another story entirely. He was a dog who didn't deal well with anything out of the ordinary. He would just "go away" mentally...it was if shutters dropped over his eyes. Oscar didn't want to be touched, he wasn't food motivated, and he didn't want to do anything that he felt might be stressful or frightening. I have never worked with such a challenging dog. It took Kevin and me a long time to build enough of a relationship with him to start working on training cues. And it took more than one attempt to get the little stinker through his CGC test.

Oscar was the first of the Vicktory Dogs to pass his CGC, back in 2008, but the court had ruled that the dogs had to pass the test within 6 months of adoption. In order to have a chance to go home, Oscar needed to pass it again. The biggest issue was that

Oscar was stubborn, and would just ignore any request he didn't want to follow. We practiced for weeks. He was notorious for heading straight to you on the "come" command, and then veering away at the last moment. We called it his "drive-by". He really didn't like the feel of sand on his tummy, so the "down" command was always an iffie proposition.

During his actual CGC test he had passed 9 out of 10 requirements. The only hurdle left was the "down". I put him in a sit, looked him in the eye, and said "Oscar, down". He turned his head away and yawned. My heart sunk....I knew I had just lost him...he had checked out. But amazingly enough, he turned back to me, and sank into the down position. He had just passed his CGC!

Within a few weeks of Oscar's CGC victory, we found out that he had been approved to be adopted by Rachel, and that she would be coming to spend time with him the next week. What a whirlwind mix of emotions that stirred up: joy that our boy was finding a home, pride that he had come so far that it was even a possibility, uncertainty that Rachel would appreciate who he was, and grief at losing a companion we had come to dearly love. To prepare Rachel for a dog who was so stoic and undemonstrative, I wrote her this letter:

My Time with Oscar

When Oscar first started coming to Parrot Garden we had to carry him in to the building. He would freeze and stare out the door, waiting to get out of here. He wouldn't eat anything, and wouldn't interact with anyone. It was very sad to watch him so shut down.

When he moved to Parrots fulltime, he spent all of his time in a corner, or under my desk. We'd have to leash him and pull on the leash to get him out to go for a walk. He refused to eat in front of us, and I'd have to leave his food in the evening, so that he could eat once we were all gone. If I touched him, his skin would twitch like a horse with a fly on its back. He refused to make eye contact with me, and would stare off into the distance if I even looked at him.

Taking him for walks could be an exercise in futility. He would walk 2 or 3 steps and then just stop. The only way to get him going again would be to pick him up and set him down again a few steps later, or to pull him a step or two. If there were people in sight, nothing could convince him to walk in that direction.

Slowly, over time, these behaviors started to change. He now runs to me in the morning for a good butt scratch. He goes for walks with Kevin without hesitation. He will even take treats from strangers. He is still very scared and shut down if he doesn't know a person, but the time it takes to get comfortable has gone from weeks to a few days.

It will take Oscar some time to get comfortable in new surroundings. He is very nervous and unsure of anything new. It will take him a few weeks to know someone enough to trust and respond to them. But this is a wonderful dog, who truly deserves a home of his own. I can't tell you how amazing he is.

There are a few things to keep in mind about Oscar:

- He is scared to death of cameras. Even if he is with someone he loves and trusts, cameras (even cellphone cameras) cause him to flee instantly.
- Oscar has absolutely NO aggression. When he is uncomfortable, he just "goes away" mentally. You can see that he has checked out.
- Oscar likes to have a safe place to hide. I have never had a problem getting him out of these safe places, although sometimes you have to pull him. Again, he shows NO aggression.
- Oscar loves car rides. The problem is getting him out of the car at the end of the ride!
- Crowds and groups of people terrify him
- He loves the packaged bones that you can get at Pet Stores
- He loves to destroy stuffed animals.
- He prefers jerky type treats to biscuit treats.
- He loves a fluffy bed.
- His favorite way of being petted is a butt scratch, followed by a body

massage. He is not all that fond of being petted on the head, unless he really trusts you.

- *He does love to tear up paper and will pull files off my desk to tear them up. Garbage cans are another favorite.*
- *He has only had one accident in my office, and that was when it was storming, and I think he was afraid to go outside.*
- *He hates bread or a lot of other things that most dogs like. But he will do anything for cheese.*
- *Loud noises bother him a lot.*

Thank you for being willing to give Oscar a chance. It will take a while for him to respond to you, but once he does, it is amazing. I have never felt so honored as the day he came to me for affection. This is a remarkable dog who we love very much.

I shouldn't have worried. Rachel was the perfect person to adopt Oscar. She was a first time dog owner, and had no pre-conceived notions of how a dog should act. The day she came to meet us was the day she became family. Rachel is more than a friend, and we will always appreciate the fact that she was willing to involve us in Oscar's successes and struggles.

Until the end of his days Oscar was never a "normal" dog. He wasn't exuberant or outgoing. He made dog friends much easier than human friends. But there is no doubt he loved Rachel and she adored her "Potato".

Kevin and I had the chance to spend the night at Rachel's house one time when we were coming home from South Dakota. We could tell that Oscar remembered us fondly, but he wasn't our boy any more. He was 100% Rachel's boy. And that is exactly the way it should be.

Because of Layla's issues with unfamiliar settings, we decided to do her CGC test in the parking lot of Parrots. She was so comfortable there that she would be able to concentrate on the test, instead of being fearful of the environment.

Two nights before her test I suddenly sat bolt upright in bed. We had spent so much time working on her problem areas (meeting other dogs, walking on a loose leash) that I had totally neglected to teach her "stay". A dog must pass every single item on the CGC test in order to pass. We had less than 48 hours to learn a new skill. The next day we started 5 minute training sessions once an hour. By the end of the day she had stay down as if she had been doing it her whole life. Layla is one smart cookie!

Unlike Oscar, who was terrified of people he didn't know...or even more than a couple of people he DID know, Layla was a social butterfly. She likes nothing more than playing to a crowd. So for her CGC we invited anyone who would like to observe a CGC test. The Parrots parking lot was lined with people. And Layla performed like a pro, prancing around the parking lot, grinning at all the familiar faces.

Kevin and I tagged teamed as handlers for her test. Since the two of them had worked so hard to become used to walking around other dogs, Kevin took her through that part of the test. And I handled the tasks that Layla and I had worked together on.

During one part of the test you have to drop the leash, put the dog in a stay, and walk away. Once you are the prescribed distance away you ask the dog to "come". Thankfully I wasn't aware of it at the time, but a flock of turkeys was wandering around behind me. I'm still surprised that our exuberant girl didn't take off after them for a joyous chase. There was no doubt that Layla rocked the test, and earned her Good Citizen certificate.

In March of 2013, the families of adopted Vicktory Dogs decided to hold a reunion at the sanctuary. Six of the dogs and their families, complete with children and other dogs, gathered together to celebrate the dog's successful transition to family pets. Because Layla had just passed her CGC, Kevin and I were invited to bring her to the ceremony, and introduce her as being newly available for adoption. One of the people Layla met that day was Tess. Tess was just getting ready to do a five week animal care internship at the sanctuary, and asked if she could visit Layla on her off-time. She made it a point to spend time with Layla every week, taking her on outings and sleep-overs. By the time she officially applied to adopt our girl, we knew it was a perfect fit. Layla was still somewhat dog reactive and had a high prey drive. Tess had no other pets, and Layla could be the pampered darling she always thought she should be. Tess has become family too. She would tell Layla that I am her Jacque Mama, and Kevin is her Papa Kevin. I am so thankful that she considers us part of Layla's extended family.

One time Layla and Tess came to visit us, and bring us a wind-chime in Ray's memory. While they were here at the sanctuary they took part in a public function for Discovery Week. Layla handled the attention like a pro. It's hard to remember when we had to carry her outside. Tess has done a remarkable job of helping Layla continue to grow.

Except for her dog issues, Layla would have made the most incredible therapy dog. She was intuitive in the way she dealt with each individual person. Tess tried so hard to get her through the training, but Layla could never get past the fact that other dogs had been very dangerous in her experience.

Tess lost Layla just over a year ago. I cried when I opened a box Tess sent me and found the blanket, bowl and "I'm a Goof" collar tag (which Oscar's mom had given her), all items I had sent her home with to begin her life as a pampered darling.

MEETING RAY

Before the Best Friends new medical building was constructed, the sanctuary clinic was located in the same building as Dog Headquarters. Dog caregivers would bring shy or scared dogs to HQ to interact with visitors and volunteers. So it wasn't unusual to see dogs hanging around the lobby.

Shortly before Layla's adoption, I went to the clinic to pick up one of her prescriptions (Layla has arthritis in her legs). As I was waiting my turn at the counter, I

turned around and saw several caregivers clustered around a little brown dog. When he turned towards me I was shocked to see a face that was so similar to Layla's.

Of course, I had to go over and see who this little pocket pittie was. Best Friends utilizes a three color collar system: green means good with anyone, purple means adults only, and red means staff only. And there was no doubt this kid was sporting a red collar. But, I was staff, so I didn't hesitate to go over and say hello. I asked Erin who she had, and she told me Ray, and that he was another one of the Vicktory Dogs, possibly Layla's and Oscar's brother.

When the Vick dogs were rescued it was pretty apparent that Ray, Oscar and Layla were related, and it was also obvious from their behavior that they were scrappy little fighters. So the evaluators named them after famous boxers: Oscar De La Hoya, Sugar Ray Leonard, and Layla Ali.

I asked about the red collar, and Erin told me Ray would get so excited to see someone he would get "mouthy"...not from aggression, but from sheer exuberance.

I knelt down on the floor and Ray came right to me. He sat his butt down on my lap, and I fell in love. I immediately contacted Michelle and told her Ray needed to be my next office dog. There was just something about this boy who loved people so much he couldn't contain himself. He had a little of glint of the devil in his eyes, and I have always been a sucker for the bad boys.

I told Kevin about this naughty little brown dog who I thought should be our next project. He was working afternoons at Dogs, so he made it a point to go meet Ray. The caregiver handed him a leash and told him to get Ray out of his run for a walk. Kevin asked Ray to sit on his bed and opened the gate to step in to leash him up. Ray jumped up, grabbed a mouth full of Kevin's shirt, and the leash and bolted out the dog door. Kevin said Ray was looking over his shoulder grinning at him as he made his escape. Ray's caregiver just laughed and told Kevin that meant Ray liked him. Ray only tortured people he really enjoyed.

Since Layla had not yet gone home, Kevin and I took turns taking Ray on outings over the lunch hour. That way we would already have a relationship when he moved to Parrots. We were hoping that would make the transition much easier than it had been for Oscar or Layla.

The first time I went to get him on my own, I remembered Kevin's experience, and the words of warning his caregiver had shared. I asked him to sit on his bed before I opened his gate. I was supposed to close the door and back away if Ray broke his sit. I swear it took me 10 minutes of trial and error before Ray sat still long enough for me to step in. Then he promptly jumped up, bit my shirt (not hard...it wasn't aggression) and took off running. Ray had a huge sense of humor and he loved to initiate new-comers to his world. I think this was actually his concept of tag.

Ray was a happy dog. He had caregivers who adored him. He had his special friend Tom who took him on outings and sleep-overs. And he had a safe, familiar place to live, with a dependable routine. There was no doubt he was a staff favorite. It was hard to meet this dog who had such a zest for life without falling for him.

So why did we want to take him on as a project and upset his routine? Because we both felt this dog deserved a chance to go home. We wanted to know he would someday be able to sleep on a couch and have zoomies in a home of his own.

I was warned that Ray could be more than a little stubborn, and if you did something to offend him, he would never forgive you. This boy could hold a grudge with the best of them.

When he first arrived at Best Friends, caregiver Jake took him out for a walk. It was winter and Jake slipped on the ice and fell, scaring Ray almost to death. Ray never, ever forgave Jake and would bark if he saw him, even if Jake was across a parking lot. Scaring

Ray was apparently unforgivable.

In a similiar situation, one of the gentlest and kindest caregivers at DogTown was named Paul. He has an energy that the dogs all respond so well to. He has a natural gift for working with troubled dog. None of that mattered to Ray. Paul had offended Ray when they first met, and he never forgave him.

Shortly after Ray had arrived at DogTown Paul decided to take him to one of the sanctuary's dog parks to have a chance to run and stretch his legs. Ray willing got in the golfcart and rode with Paul to the park. When they got inside the gate and Paul had secured it, he took Ray's leash off and attached a long-line, which is a 20 foot leash that is used to make sure you are able to retrieve a shy dog who might not want to come to you. He let Ray go, and our little brown dog took off like a rocket. Paul ran along behind just so he could help out if the line got snagged or Ray got into trouble. In Ray's little doggie mind Paul wasn't running with him, he was chasing him. It caused him so much fear and panic that he could never see Paul without barking and letting him know to stay the heck away from him. In fact, the week before his death, Ray saw Paul at a meeting at the Village. The only way we could Ray to stop bark was to block his view of Paul.

Two of the best dog people I know...but they had offended or scared Ray and he wasn't ever going to let them forget it. Good thing to know if we were going to build a relationship with this boy.

MOVING TO PARROTS

Once Layla and Tess became a family, and Layla went home, we decided to move Ray over to Parrots. It was an unmitigated disaster. Ray hated it at Parrots. He spent most of his time trying to escape, or climbing on top of things, trying to get away from the noise and chaos.

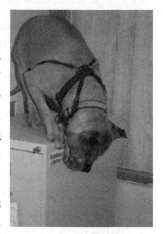

I broke out all of our tried and true methods of making a dog comfortable in a strange environment. And none of them worked. While all of the dogs started out frightened in my office, you could see them getting more and more acclimated every day. Ray not only didn't improve, he got worse. Every single day he became more panicked and unhappy. I can handle the dogs who started out rough and then became comfortable. I couldn't handle seeing a dog who was so obviously unhappy.

Ray would climb to the highest point of the room, on top of my desk, the file cabinets, and even plastic bins. He would scratch at the floor obsessively, trying to dig out. And he would try and climb though my window to get away. It wasn't that he just didn't like Parrots.....he HATED Parrots.

Our favorite trainer Tamara had moved back home, leaving a big hole in our lives. She always had the right approach to show a dog he/she was safe. Without her guidance, I was not helping Ray at all. Our new trainer Cheri was terrific, but she didn't have the years of relationship building that Tamara had with Ray

It was sobering to come to the conclusion that I had actually ruined Ray's quality of life. It was a devastating realization.

So, with a heavy heart, I returned Ray to DogTown. But this time, something was different. This time the office dog had captured our hearts.

BACK TO DOGS

To Ray's relief, we moved him back to his familiar run at DogTown. You could see how happy he was to be back in the place where he knew the routine. Everything happened at the same time every day. He saw the same people, he ate the same food, he fenced with the same dogs. Ray was a dog who NEEDED a routine to feel comfortable.

But Kevin and I had fallen in love with this naughty little dog, and neither one of us was willing to give up on him. We arranged our schedules so we could both spend time with him. I would take him to work with the trainers, to help him learn the commands he needed to know for the CGC. Kevin walked him and took him on outings. Every day either Kevin or I spent time with Ray. When he saw or heard our car he would beginning zooming around his run. And each day the bond between us became a little stronger.

Ray had many of the same training issues as his sister Layla. He lacked leash manners; walking him at first was a series of stops and starts He was just so exuberant; he wanted to pull us along with him. It took a lot of work and practice to learn to walk nicely on a leash. But it is a requirement for passing the CGC. If Ray wanted to go home, he needed to learn.

Ray was also somewhat reactive to dogs. Not as much as Layla had been…but he definitely had issues. Most of his problem was based in fear. Every dog he had ever had experience with wanted to kill him. It was much safer to act tough, and try to scare the strange dogs away.

This was a behavior Kevin had experience with and he knew exactly what to do. He drafted other staff to help by bringing dogs to walk with Ray. Parallel walks were an easy way for Ray to start getting comfortable in the presence of other dogs.

FIRST CGC TEST

After months of working together, we decided to give the Canine Good Citizenship
Test a shot. Even if he didn't pass it, it
would help us pinpoint what behaviors
needed work.

Kevin was the handler, and I was an observer. We had brought
our black lab Lucy from home, to serve as the strange dog during
the "Meet a Dog" portion of the test. To our surprise, our usually
mild-mannered Lab was extremely reactive to Ray when she met
him. Her aggressive reaction was enough to throw him off his
game.

He failed basically every single item on the practice test. He
yanked on the leash, he was reactive to the dog we brought in to
replace Lucy. He wouldn't sit, stay or come. It was disappointing,
but we knew what to work on now.....everything.

Through the entire experience Ray retained his good natured
goofiness. He was perfectly happy to be with us, and to greet the
people involved. He just had no intention of following any commands.

We gave Ray his treats, let him run around for awhile, and then
took him back to his run. Then his trainer, Kevin and I sat down
and came up with an action plan. It was up to us to figure out a
way to motivate Ray to WANT to follow our lead. The failure was
never his.....it was ours. We hadn't yet found a way to make doing
things our way more rewarding than doing things his way.

CGC SUCCESS

Two weeks later, we decided to try again. This time I was the handler. My hyper personality worked to get Ray excited and hold his attention, both important if he was going to do well on the test.

You are unable to use treats during the Canine Good Citizenship test, but we had been practicing the test and giving jackpot rewards at the end. I had a pocket full of chicken strips, and Ray knew it. I was able to keep his attention on me the entire time because he could smell that delectable scent of chicken wafting from my pockets.

We had several interns standing by to do the crowd portion of the tests, but we decided it was most important to get the dog meet and greet out of the way first. If Ray didn't pass that portion of the test, there was no sense in proceeding. To my utter shock and delighted amazement, Ray took no notice of the dog and never took his eyes off of my face.

Our little brown dog quickly passed one test item after another until the end. I looked at Cheri to see her reaction. This was the very first test that she was officiating at, and I knew she wanted there to be no doubt that Ray had passed it by the book. I raised my eyebrows and
waited for her decision. "We should have filmed that" she said, "It was textbook perfect".

When a DogTown dog passed his CGC, the evaluator goes on the

DogTown radio and announces it. I was in tears as I heard Cheri say "Attention DogTown. Ray has passed his CGC". And then we all laughed when Ray's special caregiver friend Tom came back over the radio with disbelief in his voice "Ray? Ray passed his CGC?". Yes, yes he had and we were all on top of the moon. This meant our little brown dog could finally be adopted.

HOMECOMING

Once Ray passed his Canine Good Citizenship test, he was eligible to be adopted. But we were unable to put in an application to adopt him at that time due to a very specific agreement. When the Vick dogs were accepted at the sanctuary, it was the very first time that fighting dogs had ever been rescued. No one really knew what to expect. Was BFAS admitting 22 killer dogs who would escape, terrorize the community and kill off livestock? There was more than a little local discomfort at the idea. So Best Friends told the sheriff that they would never adopt the dogs into Kane County. Kane County is enormous: 4108 square miles. Bigger than some states. That agreement gave the sheriff and the local residents a degree of comfort.

If we were serious about adopting Ray we would need to either quit our jobs and move away, or find someplace to live outside of Kane County. Really, the only option open to us was to move across the state border into Arizona. Fredonia, AZ is only about 5 miles from Kanab, but it is a tiny town, with few housing options. It was going to take some work to find a place to live in a community where Ray would be allowed.

We finally found a house with the requisite 6 foot fencing, at least in a portion of the yard, that would work for Ray and for us. The only problem was, the owner was adamant that adopters couldn't have more than 1 pet. We had another dog and seven very vocal parrots. It took some heavy negotiating, a triple deposit, and an additional $200 a month in rent, but they finally agreed to lease to us.

We promptly applied to adopt Ray and on August 14th he came home to start his mandatory six-month foster period. I told him he was the most expensive foster dog in history. I also told him that he would never live anywhere else again. I knew how important a regular routine was to this dog.

Ray had a lot to learn about being in a house. He had never been housebroken, never heard a vacuum cleaner, never stepped on carpeting. He wasn't sure about many of the noises in the house: the dishwasher, washing machine and dryer were all somewhat concerning to him. We made sure and let him explore his new enviroment until he became more comfortable.

The first six months were challenging for all of us. Ray showed a destructive side that I was unprepared for. He tore carpeting off the floor, messed up a set of blinds, and chewed through the bottom of a door.

Slowly we worked together to learn the rules of living in a house. I couldn't blame the little guy. He'd spent his first couple years chained a clearing, and the next few living in a dog run. A house was totally foreign territory. But he learned. Kindness and patience helped him figure it out.

We also found out just how sound sensitive Ray could be. One time our neighbor burned creosote soaked wood, which caused the neighborhood to fill up with smoke, and set off the smoke detectors in the house. The sound made Ray panic, and he burst out of his room, through the door to the garage, and scaled the storage shelves to the top shelf, which was well over six feet off the ground. It took some major coaxing to get our boy down . In his world, bells, beeps, and buzzers meant that he was going to be forced into a fighting situation. He wanted no part of that old life.

His sound sensitivity was so strong that I couldn't even watch the "Biggest Loser" show unless I muted the tv for the weigh-in scenes. That beep-beep-beep as the scale calibrated had him trying to climb out a window.

The only other real problem we had with Ray was his absolute greed for pizza and pizza "bones" (crust). The sanctuary is about a 10 minute drive from town and I would sometimes call in a pizza to pick up as we passed by Pizza Hut on our way home. We's stop at the drive -in window to pick up the pizza and I'd have to pop the trunk and get out of the car to put our pizza in the trunk. It was the only way I was going to get that pizza home uneaten. Nothing in the world could deter Ray once he got something in his head. He was so tenacious that he would chew through his leash to get at something he wanted. If Kevin and I wanted dinner, any take out food better be safely stowed in the trunk, or it was history!

ADOPTION DAY

And then suddenly, the six months were up. We could finally sign official adoption papers and Ray would become a permanent member of our family.

We went to DogTown headquarters to sign the official papers that would make Ray an official Johnson.

It was a big deal. We invited all of Ray's special friends to participate. The sanctuary provided a videographer to capture every moment. It was right after lunch, so the lobby was also full of volunteers waiting to sign up for their afternoon shift. Most of them seemed to be thrilled to be witnessing this special occasion.

After everyone arrived we all trooped back to the staff room to actually sign the papers. Kevin signed first as Ray and I sat on the floor and talked to his caregivers.

And when it came time to sign, I made sure Ray pawtagraphed his copy of the paperwork as well.

I cried several times that day. To see how happy every one was that Ray was in a home and loved. His former caregivers made the day very special for him and he received all the attention his little heart craved.

To Ray it was just a day where he got to see all of his

favorite people and got to have extra spe- 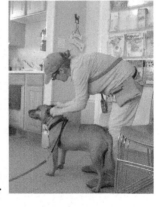 cial treats. To Kevin and I it was a milestone day that we had worked so long to achieve. I still remember Tom saying "Ok, now tell me how in the heck you got him through his CGC". I had to laugh and tell him Ray was more concerned with the chicken in my pocket than the dog walking past him.

We finished the day at the beautiful Angel's Landing, a natural amphitheater formed of Utah's red rock, while a photographer took our first official portraits as a family.

HOARDING & STUFFIES

Ray adored tearing apart his stuffies more than almost anything else in the world. We made sure he always had a full toy box of puzzle toys, balls and chewies, but stuffed toys are what he loved the best. His favorite day of the month was the day we picked up his BarkBox at the post office, because he knew there were two new stuffies in that box just waiting to be dismembered.

Although Ray had his own room he also had a crate inside his room, and that was where all his favorite treasures were stashed. Anything that was super important to him would be buried under his blankets.

It took me a little while to catch on to this quirk. It wasn't until things started going missing around the house that I got inside of his crate to look and see what was going on. He had stashed everything from clothes to a toilet brush in there. Until the day he died he would continue to hoard his favorite items.

I think life at the end of a chain in an open clearing, and then life at the sanctuary in a dog run with few toys or belongs taught Ray that if he wanted to keep something, he'd better hide it. I found it to be endearing but also a little sad. Did he really not trust that the good things would continue?

BACK AT PARROTS

Once we had taken Ray home, he and I formed a very intense bond. I've never felt quite that strong a connection to any other living being. I called him my heart dog, because it felt like he was a piece of my soul living in dog form. One that I hadn't realized I was missing until I found him.

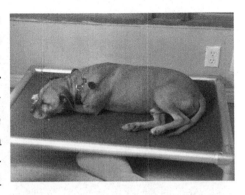

Because we were both happiest when we were together, I decided to try taking him to work with me again. I knew Parrots had been very stressful before, but now we had a much different relationship. To my joy, Ray took to Parrots as it was his own kingdom now.

He loved being the center of attention. He adored having volunteers and visitors stop by to see him. He thought our golf cart rides were the best thing ever. And he cherished our daily walk down to the village to get the mail. But best of all he loved having lunch on the deck. Because everyone would make sure and give him lots of attention and butt scratches.

Because Ray was now my dog I was able to allow people I trusted to take him on car rides and outings. Visitors would take him for walks or just to sit and pet him in my office. Many volunteers did not have an opportunity to meet any of the other Vicktory Dogs, but Ray was thrilled to meet each and every one of them. He never refused an opportunity to prove just how special he was.

He especially loved it when the children from Best Friends Kids Camp would stop by Parrots with their counselor Keeli. He always loved small people and treasured their attentions.

TRAVELING WITH MOM

Ray was made for the life of a jet-setting celebrity. He loved to have people dote on him and give him attention. For a dog who had started out so timid, he became very outgoing as long as one of his people was with him.

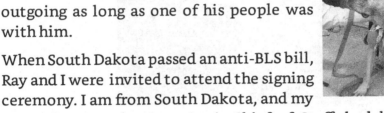

When South Dakota passed an anti-BLS bill, Ray and I were invited to attend the signing ceremony. I am from South Dakota, and my son, who was the Governor's Chief of Staff, had helped Best Friends get the bill through legislature.

This was Ray's first trip by plane and I was somewhat concerned about how he would do. I received permission to allow him to fly in the cabin with me so at least he wouldn't be in the dark and scary hold of the plane. To my surprise, Ray took to flying without any issue at all. As far as he was concerned, it was no different than riding in a car or his beloved golf cart.

We flew in to Rapid City and stayed at an old-fashioned hotel in downtown. Ray loved everything about the trip except for the city streets. It took a lot of convincing to get him to do his business on tiny scraps of grass along the road, with traffic going everywhere.

But the hotel was an experience he relished. He would strut through the lobby with his head held high, making a bee-line for a favorite desk clerk or parking valet.

There was one unpleasant occurrence at the Hotel Alex Johnson. Ray and I left our room and headed for the elevator. Ray was prancing along, because he knew his favorite desk clerk would be downstairs, ready to make a big deal over him. I had just pushed the down button to call the elevator when two giant German Shorthair Pointers came running down the hall towards us. I started screaming "no" and trying to back away from them but they just kept coming. I scooped Ray up off the floor and went running for my room. I didn't have my key card ready and I ended up pushed up against my door with my back to the on-coming dogs, to protect Ray. I was still hollering "no" as loud as I could.

After what seemed an eternity a man rounded the corner and started laughing at the scene. He said "These two goobers just want to meet your dog, they aren't going to hurt him any." And I promptly lost it. I gave him a tongue-lashing that he won't soon forget. I didn't care if his dogs were friendly, Ray wasn't with unfamiliar dogs who bum rushed him, and if there had been a fight there would have been ramifications for ALL fighting dogs. Having Ray get in a dog fight was not a possibility, ever.

While we were in Rapid we were interviewed by the local paper and made the front page, above the fold. For a former journalism student that was thrilling to me. Ray didn't seem to much care whether he got good press or not. Everything was something new to experience and enjoy and being a darling of the press was just one more way to charm his public.

There is one thing that was a little humorous. Ray was used to being a big deal to the people in his world. In South Dakota, except for a few public events, he was just another dog. He seemed to be a little disconcerted by the sheer number of people who would pass him by without a greeting. He'd look at me with questions in his eyes. Why didn't these people act that way they were supposed to, and give him attention and butt scratches?

Ray got to go wading in the Missouri River and was able to meet some of my kids and grandkids. He stayed in several new motels and never showed any nervousness or fear of a new enviroment.

However, he made sure to make our trip home memorable. Our flight was delayed due to high winds at the Las Vegas airport. We ended up sitting on the ground in St George, Utah for a couple of hours before we received the okay to proceed to Vegas. Due to the delay Ray and I missed the last shuttle back to St George. As soon as we got off the plane I started calling around for an afford-able hotel room. Best Friends has a corporate relationship with La Quinta, so I called there first. Because it was the Fourth of July, Vegas was booked solid. The only room left at the motel was a suite. Ray and I were both exhausted so I went ahead and booked the room, even though it was more expensive than I expected.

LaQuinta is very pet friendly, but the desk clerk made sure I knew that dogs were not allowed in the pool (duh) or the whirlpool tubs. I laughed and say "Ray doesn't much care for water, that won't be a problem". Famous last words.

We got settled in the room and I decided to try the big tub in the middle of the room. I was allowing it to fill while I was on the phone with the front desk, arranging a shuttle ride for the next morning when I heard a loud splash behind me. I turned around and Ray was happily paddling around in the enormous tub. It took every towel in the room and about an hour with the hair dryer to get him dry enough to sleep on the bed! That was the one and only time Ray ever willing got into a tub. I think he was just letting the desk clerk know he couldn't be bossed around!

For a dog with such a rough start, Ray became very open and accepting of new situations, as long as there were no loud beeps or bells associated with the experience. For his entire life, the sound of a bell would cause him to panic and do everything he could to escape.

But for some reason, the beeps and buzzers at the airport didn't seem to faze him in the least. Maybe because it was so crowded and there was so much other stimuli that the sounds didn't stand out

VILLAGE FRIENDS

When the weather was nice, Ray and I liked to go to lunch at the village, which is the Sanctuary's lunch room. There is a beautiful deck where we could enjoy the view, and Ray got the chance to meet new people (one of his favorite things).

Each day Ray made it a point to go up to each person dining to say "hello". I think on some level he believed that all these people are here to see him. And surprisingly enough, many were!

There is no way to overstate how important the Vicktory Dogs were to people in the rescue world. They had literally changed the face of rescue for fighting dogs. Because of their success, thousands of dogs got a second chance at life. But opportunities to actually meet, let alone touch the dogs were few and only open to a limited number of people. Ray was more than happy to stand in for all his rescued brothers and sisters.

Over the years Ray met hundreds of people and had his picture taken countless times. He was an amazing ambassador for the breed.

We sent out a request for pictures from his fans on Ray's Facebook page (Ray the Vicktory Dog) and dozens of friends sent photos of Ray and themselves, along with permission to use them in this book.

Each person Ray met and charmed carried that joy away with them. They saw first hand how a dog can recover from the most horrific experiences, if they are treated with love and consistency.

When the weather was bad, I could tell Ray was unhappy not to have his lunch on the deck. I think he really looked forward to the love and attention he got from everyone he met.

OUTING FRIENDS

Although the Village was Ray's happiest place, he was also willing to meet people at Parrots, or in the parking lot...or wherever else he came upon them.

Ray internalized the belief that every single person he met wished him well. He expected only good things from them and reacted accordingly. In his world, people mean love and security.

I think that was one of the most amazing things about this little dog. Regardless of his past, he was willing to think the best of us.

CAR RIDE FRIENDS

Ray absolutely adored riding in any type of vehicle. I wondered at that, since he hadn't had much opportunity to be in a car until he came to the sanctuary. But almost all the VDogs adored golf cart and car rides. I think it's because nothing bad or scary had  ever happened to them in vehicles. There were no bad memories to get past, only happy times.

And because car rides were such a joy for him, I would sometimes let special volunteers or friends take Ray for a ride. It was an easy way for people to spend quality time with him, while he got to enjoy a very favorite pastime.

Ray's special friend Tom the DogTown caregiver made it a point to pick him up and take him for car outings once a week or so on his lunch hour. They had a special relationship for many years, and I wanted to make sure they got to continue it, uninterrupted. I know Tom appreciated our efforts to keep him in Ray's life.

THE CHIMES

There is a legend at the sanctuary where I worked that centers around the loss of an animal. Our memorial park where our beloved family members are placed is covered in windchimes; literally hundreds of matching wind-chimes. Most of them are hung in memory of a special animal.

Whenever we have a placement ceremony (funeral), it doesn't matter how still the day is. At some point in the service or immediately following it, at least one wind-chime will ring. I have never attended a service where the beautiful tinkling song of the chimes didn't mark the occasion. Not once. I have heard that haunting tinkle every single time.

The story we tell is that when the animal crosses the Rainbow Bridge, they are young, happy and healthy again. They are so full of love and energy, so excited to see old friends, that they jump and twirl and run, building up a wind which blows over the Rainbow Bridge and comes down to earth to ring the chimes.

The Vicktory Family has a tradition of giving each other windchimes when our beloved dogs pass. It started when Roo and Clara Yori lost Hector. We wanted something to mark his passing, something that was as solid and resilient as the dogs themselves. Vicktory Dog Layla's mom Tess had a friend who makes windchimes out of steel plates and solder. The chimes are heavy; so heavy that it takes a substantial wind to bring out their voice. As each of the Vicktory Dogs comes to the end of their journey, a chime is sent to the grieving family. Ray's hangs outside my bedroom window. I miss our boy desperately, but on windy nights I can hear the song of his chimes, reminding me that we will see each other again.

RAY'S HEALTH

Ray had only been home for about a year when I noticed that he was really slowing down. He didn't move as quickly, his tail didn't wag as hard, he just seemed off.

After visiting with the medical staff at Best Friends clinic, we decided he was having a babesia flare-up and was going to require treatment. Babesia treatment is extremely expensive and takes weeks of daily medication. The drugs are so expensive that many people decide to forego treatment and have their dog humanely euthanized instead. That was not an option for us.  Ray deserved the chance to have a chance at good health.

We were extremely lucky because the clinic had treated several of the Vick dogs for babesia, and the meds they had on hand were getting ready to expire within just a couple of weeks. They let us have them for Ray at a deeply discounted rate.

Ray completed his babesia treatment and for awhile seemed to be improving. But slowly his symptoms started getting worse again. He just had no pep in his step and didn't seem to have much of an interest in anything.

Back to his doctors we went. They did blood tests, xrays, and an ultrasound. Ray was extremely anemic, and his spleen was showing nodules and masses. He was obviously losing blood somewhere, and both of his regular doctors were sure it was due to the diseased spleen. The only chance they could offer was a splenectomy, which might buy him a couple more years of a quality life.

On May 15th I dropped Ray off at the clinic on my way to work. I wasn't sure what time his surgery was going to be, as it was a spay/neuter day and the clinic was busy. Dr. Chris assured me she'd call me after the surgery was complete.

At about 4:00 Dr Chris called and said Ray had come through surgery with flying colors. She said he was already coming out of anesthesia and seemed to be doing great. We talked about how nasty his spleen looked and that she really thought we should send it in for pathology testing just to be sure. I asked if I could stop and see him on the way home and she convinced me he was still so out of it he wouldn't even know I was there. She assured me I could pick him up in the morning and take him home.

I called and let Kevin know that surgery was successful and we had a lovely celebratory dinner. That night, at 11:05 pm my phone rang. When I picked it up and saw the clinic was calling my heart sank. I knew before I even answered. When I said hello, Dr Chris was on the line. She let me know that Ray had thrown a blood clot and died almost instantly. I am beyond thankful that a vet tech was there, and was able to cradle him in her arms in his final moments.

My heart shattered in that moment. I thanked Dr Chris and hung up the phone. I cannot ever remember crying harder in my life. To be honest, I even seriously considered suicide in that moment. I had just lost my heart dog and my mind was unable to handle the news. I have never loved an animal more. Even now, six years later my eyes are full of tears remembering that horrible night.

THE PLACEMENT

One of the things that is most important for anyone who lives or works at the sanctuary is making sure each animal has a placement ceremony, or funeral if you will. We gather together, have a reading and a prayer, and then people tell stories about the animal. Funny stories, sad stories.....just sharing what we knew and loved about them.

I remember very little about Ray's service. I was just shocked at how many people had taken time to come and help us grieve for our little brown dog. The stories that were shared made me laugh and cry. They told about how Ray was unable to have toys in his run because several of the Vicktory dogs had to have surgery after eating toys. Since he wasn't given anything he could tear up, he collected and hoarded the only thing he had ....poop. Every morning the caregivers would come into his run and find his dog bed piled high with poop.

After the readings and memories, each person attending takes a turn pouring a hand trowel of dirt into the grave and then the grave is filled in and tamped down. Then each person takes a brightly colored stone and sets it on the placement marker. Every time you go to visit a grave, you leave a stone. This was Ray's grave site on the day of his placement. Someone recently shared a photo with me that was taken earlier this year. Ray's marker is over-flowing with stones. It makes my heart happy to know people still remember and visit him. It would make him so happy to know they were coming to see him. He lived for people coming to see him.

I ordered his marker specially made using my favorite picture of him painted by Levity Tomkinson. We didn't know his birthday so used his rescue year. And nowhere on his plaque will you find the word Vick or Vicktory. I do not want my beloved boy going through eternity harnessed to that man's name.

LOSING A BELOVED COMPANION

Almost every day I see a Face-book post that someone's be-loved companion has passed away. Each and every time it sends a stabbing pain through my heart. I feel for their suffer-ing and wish I could ease it for them.

In just the same manner as those dealing with human loss, these loving caregivers will need to transverse the five stages of grief that Dr. Elizabeth Kubler-Ross identified in her book "On Death and Dying": denial, anger, bargaining, depression and acceptance. No one can help make the transitions easier, and each person will deal with grief in their own way and in their own time.

Those who are not "animal people" will never understand. But those who have welcomed beloved companions into their lives know all too well that the loss of a "pet" is every bit as painful as the loss of a human family member. In some cases, it is even harder.

Dogs, cats, birds, horses and all other companion animals are not just living obligations that we let into our lives. They become so much more: a friend, a companion, a soul mate. In some cases, they become just as close as our children. And their loss strikes at the center of who we are as humans.

Human children grow up, move out, and move on with their own lives. Our companions never do. They don't ask for money, or argue politics, or ask to borrow the car. They don't roll their eyes at our old-fashioned ideas as our human offspring often do. They are always glad to see us and act as if we've been gone forever each and every time we come home. They are loyal, they are loving, and they think we are absolutely wonderful just the way we are. Is it any wonder we grieve their loss so strongly?

Thankfully there are studies which validate what we are feeling. A 1988 study in the Journal of Mental Health Counseling asked dog owners to express how close their companions were to them. A majority of respondents placed their dog as close as their closest family member. In an unbelievable 38% of cases, the person responding said their dog was their closest family attachment.

A study that was published in 2002 showed that the death of a beloved companion is every bit as devastating as the loss of a spouse or significant other.

I know first hand how strong the grief can be. When Ray died it was one of the most significant losses I have ever experienced. Even today, years later, I still tear up when I think about the night we lost him. It took time and the assistance of a really good counselor for me to begin to understand.

Grief is not an emotion, it is a state of being. Sorrow will roll over us in unexpected waves. At first, it is hard to even catch a breath as we are pummeled by the tidal wave of grief. Slowly, with time, it begins to recede somewhat. But just like the tides of the ocean, it never really goes away. For the most part it becomes gentler and less devastating. But there are always those moments when we are once again pulled under by a current of pain. Eventually it becomes a constant awareness, but it no longer rules our hearts or minds.

It is so important to give yourself permission to grieve. You have lost an incredibly important emotional attachment. It doesn't matter if others understand. You need to acknowledge your loss and recognize the sorrow and emotions. Do not allow others to tell you how or how long to mourn. It is not their loss and they have no say in what you are experiencing.

I will always miss Ray. I will always have those moments when i think of him and cry. But now I can celebrate what we had together instead of just grieving his loss. And that is what I wish for all my friends and family as they experience this most painful of life's transitions.

GOOD NEWZ KENNELS

On the 10th anniversary of the Michael Vick bust a ceremony was held at the site of his former Bad Newz Kennels. When the property had come up for auction it was purchased by the organization Dogs Deserve Better and was rechristianed Good Newz Rehab Center for Chained Dogs.

The occasion was attended by many people who had been instrumental in the arrest and prosecution of the case. Vick dog adopters attended as did author Jim Gorant who penned the amazing book "The Lost Dogs" about the Vick dog bust. Everyone who had been so intimately involved with the dogs gathered to celebrate their lives and honor them.

What was once a clearing in the woods where nothing stood but barrels and heavy log-chained dogs, covered in filth, suffering the wounds of dog fighting, was now an open fenced in dog park for the dogs being rehabbed by DDB. And the organization, which hosted the event, had purchased a flowering dogwood tree for each and every dog, including the ones who never made it out alive and were found buried on the property. In the space where once dogs lived in fear and pain, abused and neglected, now trees will grow tall and strong.

I was unable to attend the event. I had no desire to see where Ray had suffered. But Kevin was able to make the pilgrimage along with Layla's and Oscar's moms, Tess and Rachel, thanks to wonderful friends who purchased t-shirts to help cover travel costs. (And thanks to Levity for designing the shirts!)

Kevin was brave enough to enter the black shed where the dogs were fought. He saw the rape-rack, blood stained walls, and hypodermic needles still laying on window sills. I do not think my heart could have handled that graphic immersion into the horror our dogs experienced.

As part of the weekend, Kevin, Tess and Rachel hung a larger version of the family wind-chimes in a tree overlooking the memorial field. The chimes were placed in honor of all the dogs, and to recognize the work DDB has done to cleanse the area of any residual evil as they work to rehabilitate other abused and neglected dogs. The chimes are incredibly solid and heavy. During the ceremony they hung still and soundless.

However, the next night a storm blew through the area. According-ing to Dogs Deserve Better then-director Denise Cohn, the chimes didn't just ring, they sang. I guess it took a day or two for all of the departed Vicktory Dogs to get together and dance in unison, because that was some wind they stirred up to let us know they are now happy and healthy, waiting for us to come together once again, on the other side of the Rainbow Bridge.

MCCAELA THE TURTLE

Because of Ray, we learned to open our hearts to pit bull type dogs who had suffered at the hands of humans. And because of the bonds we built with the other Vicktory families, McCaela the Turtle came into our lives.

I have written extensively about our dogs rescued from the world of dog fighting, but somehow Turtle often ends up in the background. And she shouldn't. Turtle is everything that is best about pit bull terrier type dogs. She has three great loves in her life, her people, food, and naps. When my husband Kevin was critically ill, Turtle never left his side and they formed an unbreakable bond. She is loyal, gentle and eager to please. She is stubborn as any mule. She is incredibly human-oriented. And her story belongs in this book as well.

On January 31, 2013, police in Toledo, Ohio entered an abandoned building on Fearing Street as part of an on-going drug investigation. They found six pit bull terrier type dogs chained to the floor. The dogs were severely under-weight, scarred and caked with urine and feces. Two of the dogs had legs that had been broken and never set. They were all full of parasites and were shy and timid with rescuers.

The dogs were held at Lucas County Canine Care and Control while the legal case made its way through the court system. After 10 long months, their abuser, Carl Steward, was found guilty of five felony counts of dogfighting and sentenced to 18 months of incarceration and five years of probation.

Ultimately, the court ruled that the dogs could be evaluated for possible rehabilitation. Up until late 2012, it was Ohio State Law that all fighting dogs were inherently vicious and must be euthanized. These were the first fighting dogs rescued since the law had been changed. They were the first to have a chance to be evaluated and possibly rehabilitated.

Jean Keating, Executive Director of the Lucas County Pit Crew (LCPC), wanted to make sure the dogs had the best possible evaluation, so she asked Donna Reynolds and Tim Racer from the California-based organization BadRap to come to Ohio and assess the dogs. After the assessments were completed, two of the dogs were determined to have been too damaged to be safe and were humanely euthanized.

That left four dogs: Honeysuckle (renamed Joy) and Butterball (renamed Georgia) both went into foster homes with LCPC. Mopsy and McCaela, who had more severe issues, would need to be placed in more specialized fosters or rescues equipped to deal with their problems. Eventually Mopsy was pulled by a rescue, which left McCaeila sitting along at the shelter.

Time was running out for McCaela. The staff at the shelter had started to call her Turtle because she loved to roll on her back for belly rubs, but couldn't easily right herself afterwards.

It is unclear why Turtle was having so much trouble finding placement. She was sweet and submissive with humans, although she did appear to have some major dog issues. Maybe it was because she had funny googly eyes, or that one of her legs had been broken and never properly set. Maybe it was because one of her ears was half torn away and the other had been shredded into ribbons. Maybe it was because all of her teeth had been broken off at the gumline, probably from trying to chew through her chain.

In truth, it was probably because she was Babesia positive. Babesia is a microscopic blood parasite that causes severe anemia. It is extremely expensive to treat and can be passed from dog to dog by deep puncture bites.

But for whatever reason, management at Lucas County Animal Control began to worry about Turtle's quality of life. After more than a year of living in a shelter environment, Turtle was beginning to show signs of stress. If placement couldn't be found soon, it might be kinder to end her suffering.

Vicktory Dog Oscar's mom Rachel Johnson had been following the Fearing Six dogs from the beginning. She had held an auction to raise funds for the dogs. She worked to get the other Vicktory parents involved in the situation. She took on these dogs as a personal crusade, and refused to give up on them.

And it's a good thing she did. Because of her efforts, Jasmine's House (a rescue established by Vick dog Jasmine's adopter) decided to pull Turtle and committed to finding her a perfect home.

Although Jasmine's House Rescue is located in Maryland, they had recently established a satellite branch in Salt Lake City with Vicktory Dog Halle's adopter Traci. Turtle was picked up at Animal Control and caught a series of rides with volunteers committed to getting her to Salt Lake City.

Turtle was quickly place in a foster home but they really didn't have the right situation for a dog with Turtle's issues. After an unfortunate event with fireworks and a neighbor dog she had to leave the foster home. It was clear that Turtle needed more rehab than the family was prepared to provide. Like many fighting dogs, Turtle is extremely sound sensitive, and fireworks, thunder, ticking or beeping sounds can make her frantic.

She ended up being boarded at a veterinary office in a stainless steel cage for a few days. Even though Kate Callahan, a Jasmine's

House representative went and walked Turtle twice a day, it was not a good situation for her, especially not after her year at the pound

Ray and I were in South Dakota participating in a celebration to mark the end of breed discrimination in the state. While we were busy at a gathering on the Capitol steps, other Vicktory parents were working behind the scenes to get Turtle home. Handsome Dan's mom Heather contacted my husband Kevin and asked if we could serve as an emergency foster for Turtle while other arrangements were pursued. Of course Kevin said yes.

The second Saturday of July in 2014, Kate and Traci drove Turtle to Kanab and we all met at the sanctuary. Kevin and I brought Ray along so we could determine if it was even feasible to bring Turtle into our house. Then we all drove home and let Turtle explore our house and yard.

It took us less than 24 hours to decide that Turtle wasn't an emergency foster, Turtle was home. We applied to adopt her on Monday morning.

Turtle and Ray were never able to interact. They both had suffered too much trauma to be able to befriend each other. Nether one had the dog skills necessary to build a stable relationship. But that was okay. Our house was divided in half as was our yard. We were able to keep both dogs happy and socialized, just separately.

In the years Turtle has been home she has blossomed. She has figured out how to play with toys, she discovered a love for chuck-it balls, and she has developed relationships with our dogs Bubba and especially with Nemo, our bottle baby adoptee. Nemo and Turtle can often be found curled on a dog bed together, licking each other's faces.

Turtle loves every person she has ever met, but she has a special love for children. She is so sweet and gentle, and wants only to spend time with any child in sight. She has always had an amazing relationship with our grandson Foster.

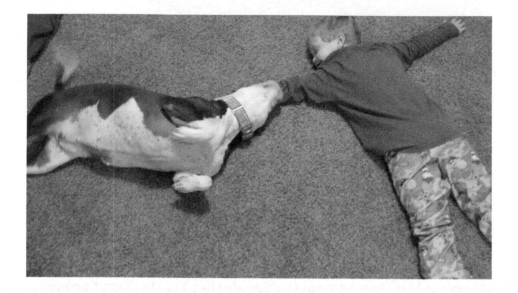

The years are catching up with our old lady of a dog. We think she is between 13 and 15 years old now. She has painful arthritis in her back end and needs to wear non-slip booties on her feet. But she is still the sweetest of all of our dogs and we are thankful for each day we have with her.

FINDING BUBBA G

Late May 2015 I was still reeling from the loss of my beloved little brown pit bull Ray. That dog went everywhere with me, and his death left me feeling bereft and distraught. It was quickly apparent that I did not have the luxury of waiting; I needed another dog in my life immediately.

Through a series of coincidences, Bubba G was brought to my attention. Oscar's mom Rachel was volunteering with a rescue in Colorado, and she had been doing some fundraising for them. I contacted the director of Coloradogs and asked if she knew of a calm male dog, who was dog friendly and eager to learn. She immediately suggested Bubba G. He had only been in her rescue for a couple of weeks, but she thought he fit my requirements in every way.

Bubba was found beside a dumpster in an alley in Denver, covered in wounds consistent with dog fighting. He was found lying on a blanket, so it was apparent someone had dumped him there. It was also clear that his injuries had been inflicted over several weeks. Some were fresh, some were healing, and some were infected. The worst and freshest of the injuries was a scalp that had been torn away from his head. The good Samaritan who found him, called Denver Animal Care and Control.

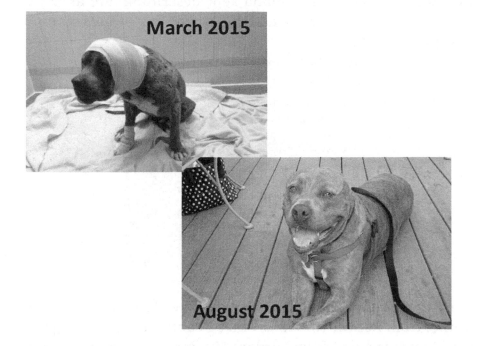

March 2015

August 2015

Bubba quickly became a favorite of the staff at the shelter. He underwent 5 separate surgeries while in their care, as they attempted to deal with the destruction of Bubba's head and ears. Unfortunately they were unable to save his ears.

Denver is a Breed Discriminatory City and has been for years. Pit bull terrier type dogs are not allowed in the city limits. But something about Bubba's demeanor and stoic acceptance of his medical care touched the staff deeply. They worked to get him healthy, and to find a rescue outside of Denver to pull him.

Bubba was pulled by Coloradogs and set about charming everyone there as well. My good friend and Oscar's mom Rachel Johnson started taking him on outings. She went out of her way to take him places to see if he had what it takes to become my constant companion. After visiting with her, I applied to adopt him, and was approved in short order. Throughout the process everyone involved with Bubba kept describing him as "a little mouthy". (I have since learned this is code for "he uses his mouth inappropriately".)

In early June a wonderful volunteer offered to drive him halfway home, from Denver to Utah. I met Deanna Sullivan at a gas station just this side of the border. My first glimpse of Bubba was shocking. I had seen pictures, and even a couple of videos, but nothing prepared me for the sheer size of this dog. He is enormous. I quickly texted my husband: "we are going to need more dog food". Ray's top weight was 42 pounds. Bubba was closer to 80 pounds.

Deanna and I visited briefly, and took the obligatory pictures of the hand-off. Just as she was getting in her car, she turned to me and said "he's a little mouthy". There was that phrase again. Just what was the big deal with this boy who was so obviously human oriented?

Bubba walked nicely on the leash as I took him to my car and loaded him into the back seat. No sooner had I gotten in the driver's side, than he jumped into the front passenger seat. OK... so this dog wants to be the navigator. That was fine with me. We pulled out, onto the interstate, and I quickly got up to speed. There we were, tooling down the highway at 80 mph when Bubba decided to climb into my lap. I used my right arm to block him and he took the entire thing, from wrist to elbow, into that enormous mouth, and then sat there grinning at me with his mouth full of my arm. I decided he might need to burn off a little energy and pulled off the next exit to take him for a walk. Yes, this boy was mouthy all right.

I had wanted a dog who would pass temperament and intelligence training to become my service dog so Bubba was evaluated the next day by the Canine's with Careers program at he sanctuary. He passed the screening and we met his trainer Keith Hightower, a positive reinforcement trainer who contracted with Best Friends to train dogs for people who needed canine assistance.

During our first training session Bubba got over-excited as he often would when too stimulated, and he kept biting me in the butt and grabbing my arm in his mouth. I looked over at Keith and caught her rolling her eyes. A year later, after Bubba had become the well-mannered gentleman he is today, I asked her about that day. I asked if she didn't think Bubba could learn what he needed to and she replied "Oh, I knew Bubba had what it took. I wasn't sure you did". As I mentioned elsewhere in this book, the majority of dog training is to teach the human half of the partnership.

Shortly after we adopted Bubba we needed to go home to South Dakota for my son's wedding. He was nowhere near ready to appear in public settings so I asked the most dedicated dog person I know if Bubba could stay with her. Justyne Moore was an important person in Ray's life. She has an amazing ability to connect with dogs, even those with major behavior issues. I knew she could cope with our naughty boy. I recently found the note I gave her along with Bubba's bags of toys, food and treats. Reading it now just makes me laugh!

Dear Justyne:

> *First off, Bubba has gotten very mouthy and jumps up to grab clothes and arms in his mouth. Do not try standing still or turning your back. He'll just bite your legs. Leave the room for a few seconds if he acts up. We are working on that, and he is being muzzled trained for those times he is showing rough play. It usually helps a lot to play ball with him when he looks like he might be getting over excited.*
> *I usually keep a spare ball on my person, so I can hand him one if I see him gearing up.*
> *Bubba needs sunscreen on the scar on his head if he is going to be out in the sun.*
> *Bubba loves bully sticks, balls and stuffed animals with squeakers. Also likes a bone before bed.*

Bubba is not overly food motivated. Sometimes takes him a couple of hours to finish a meal.

Bubba is used to being crated when we sleep or if we have to leave him.

He is very prone to chewing things up. Be careful what you allow him access to.

Bubba is not overly housebroken, but has gotten good about going when I take him out and tell him to "go potty". Pooping generally requires a walk, or he'll poop in his room (sorry).

I feed him 2 cups of dry and a half can of wet, twice a day. Use slow eat bowl to avoid bloat.

CAUTION: he likes to tip over his water bowls. I only fill his pail about 1/3 of the way, so there isn't as much mess if he dumps it.

Training class is Wednesday morning at 9:00 at the park in the Ranchos. Keith knows you will be bringing him for class. We will suspend his individual sessions while I am gone.

We usually play ball hard for about 10-15 minutes in the morning, and again in the evening before bed. You will know when he is getting done, as he'll stop bringing back the ball every time.

After a year of working with Keith, Bubba "graduated" by flying with me to Salt Lake City and attending a conference by my side. He has been my constant companion ever since.

While I worked at the sanctuary he went to work every single day with me. When we moved back to South Dakota he stayed home while I completed my probationary period. The day I was granted permanent status I started the paperwork to request him as a workplace accommodation. Bubba has the distinct honor of being the very first non-guide dog service dog ever allowed in a state government office building.

ESSAYS AND BLOG POSTS

The next section of this book is a selection of blog posts I've written over the years. I've had people ask for copies and thought that collecting here is this book was appropriate. I hadn't written anything in years when we adopted Ray. He became my muse and everything I have written since is because of the effect he had on my life. If you haven't read these articles before, I hope you enjoy them.

YES, HE'S A SERVICE DOG

Recently there has been a lot of press about fake service dogs. Articles are written about how to spot a fake service dog. What to do if you see a fake service dog. How easy it is to pretend your dog is a service dog. How to order a vest and ID card for your dog so you can pretend he is a service dog. It has become something of a cause de jour.

The only problem is, all this attention can make things much harder for people who have a legitimate need for a trained dog assistant. Especially for people who do not appear to be disabled. Here is a news flash: service dogs are not just for people who have visual impairments any more. They can be trained to help with everything from physical mobility issues to PTSD.

I have had severe anxiety my entire life. Pair that with ADHD and a tendency towards panic disorders and I can be one spastic mess of a human if I am left untreated. I have tried many medications over the years, from Ritalin to anti-depressants. In most cases the side-effects were worse than the original issues.

Unlike many people, I am not self-diagnosed. I have been under the care of doctors, therapists, psychiatrists and counselors. I was severely injured a couple of times as a child and I hid the injuries from my parents because I was worried about how they would react. My parents never laid a hand on me in anger. I had no rational basis for my fear of their reaction. It was part of my disorder.

When we adopted Ray something funny happened. He was able to sense when I was getting anxious and he would solicite my attention and break the cycle of panic. This was the first time something external had helped me break the mounting panic. I came to depend on his ability to read my emotions, monitor my breathing, and to react appropriately to help me cope. When we traveled together to South Dakota for the anti-BSL rally I learned he was even able to help me with the anxiety of flying. All without being trained. Ray was NOT a service dog, but he had instincts that would have made him an amazing one if he'd had the necessary training. Natural dog behaviors do not make a dog a service dog. They must be trained to complete tasks on cue in order to meet the legal definition of an assistance dog.

When Ray died, I realized that I had not only lost my heart dog, I had lost someone who had helped me function normally. That loss was so profound, I found myself back in counseling, trying to make sense of why my grief was so paralyzing. It was my counselor who first suggested that what Ray had provided on his own could be duplicated by a trained service dog. She wrote me a prescription for a service dog, something that is not a requirement, but which has proven to be beneficial more than once.

We adopted Bubba G specifically to train as a service dog. We went through group and individual training to teach him what he needed to know to help me with my issues. He is a natural, although some skills came harder than others. We worked on training for about 18 months before he was able to be considered a service dog. He attends work every day with me and allows me to feel as if I am a fully functional human being.

A few months ago we were walking over to McDonalds for lunch. Bubba was wearing his service dog vest (vests are not a requirement for service dogs but do make things easier with public access). An older couple walked into the building right before us. The man started to hold the door for us when his wife said something I couldn't hear and he let the door close in my face. I opened the door and told Bubba to enter. The woman spun on her heels, barged past us, saying loudly enough that everyone in the lobby could hear her " I'm not going to eat any place that allows a dog in the building". She made eye contact with me and spit out "fake service dog" before exiting the building.

I can understand the frustration with fake service dogs. I've been in Walmart when small yappy dogs are dragging their people around and snapping at people. But if you see someone with a dog who is obviously well-trained, with perfect public access manners, you cannot assume he isn't a necessary accommodation for his or her handler. And frankly, it isn't any of your business. It is up to an individual business to challenge the handler if they think something is wrong. And they can only ask if this is a service dog and what tasks has he been trained to do. If the handler can answer those questions, and the dog is behaving appropriately, the dog must be allowed anywhere the general public is able to go. If a dog is barking, soiling or marking, or acting aggressively, a business has every right to ask the handler to remove the dog.

Bubba is my best buddy. But even more importantly, he allows me to feel normal in a world that can seem hostile or overwhelming. We have been lucky in most of our public interactions, but it only takes one bad experience to increase my anxiety going forward. Please think before you accuse someone of having a fake service dog.

DOGS WHO STAND FOR SOMETHING

A few years ago, Ray and I were invited to address college students from across the country who were spending spring break volunteering at the sanctuary. They were gathered to attend a workshop presented by Ledy Van Kavage (Best Friends attorney extraordinaire!) on Breed Discrimination laws. Ray and I were the opening act. It was an opportunity to educate people about pit bull type dogs, and a reminder that not everyone knows the full story.

In April of 2007, a young man named Davon Broddie was arrested on drug charges. At that time he gave his address as a home in Surry County, Virginia, which belonged to his cousin, Atlanta Falcon's Quarterback Michael Vick: the NFL's highest paid player. When a search warrant was served to look for additional drugs, the police were surprised to find a large number of dogs. An additional search warrant was obtained to search for evidence of animal neglect or abuse. What they found left little doubt that this was a large-scale dog fighting operation: a blood stained "pit", a "rape rack", training equipment, performance enhancing drugs and dogs chained with heavy log chains, in a clearing in the woods, some with injuries consistent with dog fighting.

Fifty-one fighting dogs were seized and moved into several different municipal shelters in the area. Traditionally suspected fighting dogs were held as evidence until the trial was completed, and then euthanized. They were referred to as "kennel trash" and shelter employees tried hard not to become attached to them, given their dismal outlook for a future. Even un-weaned puppies were routinely killed as being irredeemably tainted by dog fighting.

This time things were different. A few vocal animal welfare groups, including Best Friends Animal Society, petitioned the court to have the dogs evaluated individually for possible rehabilitation. But just as vocal were the groups who maintained the dogs couldn't be saved. That they were "ticking time bombs" or "the most aggressively trained killing machines in America". Thankfully the judge decided to give the dogs at least a chance to prove themselves. He appointed Rebecca Huss as Guardian and Special Master to the court. It was her job to arrange individual evaluations for the dogs and determine each one's fate.

Teams of behavior experts from the ASPCA, BadRap from California, and Best Friends Animal Society arrived to complete the evaluation process. Each dog was to be tested for dog aggression as well as human aggression. It was hoped that two or three of the 49 surviving dogs (two died while in care) would be deemed salvageable. Imagine everyone's surprise when all but one of the dogs showed at least some degree of ability to be rehabilitated. One dog, who had been bred and fought repeatedly, was just too emotionally and physically damaged to try and save. She was humanely euthanized. The remaining 48 dogs were dispersed to 8 different rescue groups for adoption, rehabilitation or sanctuary.

Best Friends Animal Society took 22 of the most challenging dogs. The dogs who were going to need a little more help to become eligible for a home. Two of the dogs were court-ordered to remain at the sanctuary for life: Lucas, who was Bad Newz Kennel's Grand Champion and Meryl, who in her fear had snapped at her evaluator. When the dogs first came to Best Friends, caregivers and trainers were with them 24 hours a day, as everyone tried to get an idea of what this task was going to require. The dogs instantly bonded with these humans who were kind and patient. It didn't take long for staff to figure out the biggest issue with them wasn't aggression....it was fear. These dogs had lived a life that was painful and frightening. They were totally unsocialized. They had never know kindness, good food, fresh water, and a warm, safe place to sleep. They didn't know how to walk on a leash. They had never spent a night under a roof. And some of them were ill with Babesia, a blood born parasite that fighting dogs pass through deep puncture wounds. (Babesia can also be contracted by tick bites).

Some of the Vicktory Dogs (as BFAS renamed them) were able to be adopted as soon as the trainers felt they would be able to be successful in a home. Some of the dogs who were more damaged were court-ordered to complete their Canine Good Citizen (CGC) test before they could leave. The CGC is an incredibly difficult test for any dog. For dogs who were dealing with crippling fear, it takes a Herculean effort on the part of both the dog and his trainer.

One by one the dogs started passing their tests and finding wonderful homes. The court had also put some stringent requirements in place for potential adopters. Every interested person was required to pass a Federal Background Check. They had to come to the sanctuary and meet the dogs. They had to provide a home that could pass an inspection for safety and security. Yards had to be fenced with 6 foot fencing. Since these were the first fighting dogs ever saved, it was critical that they went to stable homes with people who would be willing to do what was necessary to keep the dogs safe and happy. And all the safe-guards worked. The dogs have been integrated into homes with small children, cats, and other dogs. There has never been a single issue with any of the dogs who were placed in loving homes.

The dogs acted like they were on a mission to prove to the world that they are dogs...just dogs. Not "killing machines", not aggressive, dangerous animals. Just dogs like any other dog. Dogs with individual quirks that just endear them to their families. Dogs who have become therapy dogs, agility champions, and emotional support dogs. Dogs like Cherry, who stood on a stage in New York City last year and happily met his many fans who were attending a screening of the PBS show Visionaries. Dogs like Handsome Dan, who is so amazing that he inspired his parents to start a dog rescue of their own, in his name. Dogs like Layla, who is working hard to become a certified therapy dog. Dogs like Ray, who trustingly follows me wherever I choose to take him.

Today Ray went to lunch with me on the deck of the Village Cafe. He not only tolerated the people who wanted to meet him, he actively solicited their attention. This little dog who was once so very frightened is now an ambassador for pit bulls and fighting dogs everywhere. Because of the relationship we've built, he willing tackles things that I never thought he could deal with. Last month when we arrived at the Vegas airport we had to use an escalator. I don't mind admitting that I was apprehensive approaching it. I shouldn't have been. Ray confidently stepped on, and proudly looked around as he rode to the top, where he nimbly stepped off without missing a beat. (Unlike his human mom, who always stutter steps getting off an escalator).

The Bad Newz Kennels bust, which happened more than 10 years ago and captured the attention of dog lovers all across the country, has changed the shape of the world for pit bull terrier type dogs. Dogs who are seized are now routinely assessed for rehabilitation. There is no longer a belief that these dogs are somehow responsible for the life that was forced on them. That they are damaged goods, better off dead.

The Vicktory Dogs are aging. In the past few years we have started to lose some of them. Last August Lucas, the Grand Champion (snuggle bug, lap sitting, amazing dog) passed away from complications of Babesia. We know our time with these amazing dogs is limited. Many of them are dealing with health issues directly related to the abuse they suffered. But even when they cross over the Rainbow Bridge they will continue to influence policy. These 48 dogs who have proven, beyond a shadow of a doubt, that fighting was something that was forced on them, not something they were born to do. Once they had the opportunity to become companions, they took it and ran with it. Ray's sigh when he lays his head in my lap says it all. These dogs were victims, not criminals. And because of their bravery and loving nature they have taught us all so much. If dogs like these....dogs who were trained, fought and abused.... can become loving family members, how can anyone say that pit bull type dogs are inherently dangerous? It just doesn't make sense.

I understand the anger some people feel towards the man who bankrolled Bad Newz Kennels. Their disgust that he is once again playing football and making tons of money. But frankly, I never even think about that. I know Ray doesn't. He lives totally in the moment, enjoying the good things happening in his life now. I take my cue from him. We only have so much time left to spend together, and we are going to enjoy every second of it.

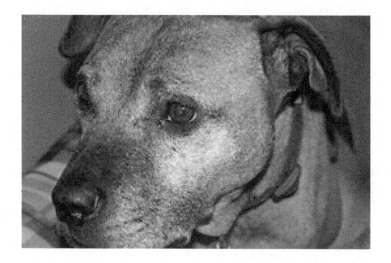

WHY A PIT BULL?

There are dozens of large dog breeds to choose from, why a pit bull?" is a question I've been asked more than once. It is a question that is impossible to answer, unless A) you are a dog lover and B) you have had the unique good fortune to have been loved by a pit bull terrier type dog.

Growing up my family had Basset Hounds. In my adult life we have had an Irish Setter, a Basenji, a Golden Retriever, a MinPin, a couple of Labs and a mutt. But that was BP (before pittie). Everyone has some particular thing they are looking for in a dog. A hunter likes a **retriever or pointer**. A rancher wants a shepherd type dog. Some people like toy breeds as they are small, portable and don't make a lot of mess.

My requirements for a dog were pretty specific: I wanted a dog who would chill out when I was lazy and willing to go when I wasn't. I wanted a dog who wanted to be with me, as much as I wanted to be with him. I wanted a dog who's joy in life is contagious. I wanted a dog who was smart enough to train but stubborn enough to be a challenge. I wanted a dog who could make me laugh. And I wanted a dog with a heart big enough to love everyone he met. No dog BP ever filled all of my requirements. They were great dogs. I loved them very much. But it seems like I was destined to always be missing something in my canine relationships.

And then I met Ray. Something changed in my life the day I met this little brown dog. He has helped me become a better person. He has shown me that there are human/canine bonds that transcend owner/pet relationships. He has forced me to become more social and to talk to strangers....something that has always been hard for me. Because of Ray, I have become more educated in positive reinforcement training and breed discrimination. Ray taught me that pit bulls are not big, scary time-bombs waiting to go off and kill someone. Ray fits every single one of my requirements for the perfect dog. And when Turtle came into our lives, she did the same thing.

DEAR PIT BULL HATERS

See this dog? This little old man of a dog? He is a pit bull terrier type dog. He is a former fighting dog. He is the stuff your insane nightmares are made of. But regardless of what you believe to be true about his breed, he is our beloved family member.

I am incredibly blessed to be able to take Ray with me to work every single day. We spend all day, every day together. He has met and charmed literally thousands of people. And never once, in all that time, has he been anything but polite and loving with everyone from littles to adults.

No matter where we go, or how we travel, Ray is always willing to meet the people who want to meet him. He doesn't know or understand that some people hate him because of his breed or how he looks. He doesn't know how many people wish he were dead. And even if he did know, I doubt he would care. His world is full of people who think he is amazing just the way he is.

Last week I watch Ray gently greet a 10 month old baby who reached out to him. He was amazingly careful with her. But you can believe both parents and I were carefully monitoring the interaction. That is what responsible people do...make sure neither was put into a dangerous situation, or one they couldn't handle.

I am horrified whenever anyone is hurt by a dog. But invariably dog aggression can be traced to either human action/inaction or a physical issue. Dogs are hardwired to please and serve us, none more than pittie type dogs. But every single time a pit bull type dog is vilified in the press, it makes one more punk want to have one. If these dogs are so bad ass that they have to be banned....that is exactly the dog they want to have. Then they mistreat, torture, starve and beat the dog. And we wonder why he becomes aggressive. According to your DBO logic, it must be the way the dog looks.

I am not a pit bull apologist. I don't care what breed of dog Ray is. He could be a poodle and I would feel the same way. I connect with who he is, not what he is. As my little brown dog's health starts to decline, it becomes even more important that I help him build a legacy. Not because he is a former Vick dog, but because he is a member of the most vilified breed of dog on earth.

Ray's time with us is limited. But one of his favorite things to do is to go the Village at lunch time, sit on the deck, and soak up love and admiration from the people around him. He expects nothing less. Because in his world he is a gentle dog with a loving soul. He is not a ticking time bomb. He is not a finely tuned killing machine. He isn't a devil dog waiting for the right moment to attack. He is a sweet and shy, funny and stubborn, wonderful old man of a dog.

One final thing for you pit bull haters. Unlike you, Ray is willing to judge people on who they are, not how they look. Maybe you could learn something from him.

WE CAN'T SAVE THEM ALL

Nor Should We Try

Note: *this is probably the hardest thing I have ever had to write. Please understand that I am not calling out or blaming any person or organization for what happened to me. And I am certainly not blaming Bosco. I just want us to be able to have healthy conversations around behavioral euthanasia. The fact is that some dogs are too damaged and/or frightened to have a decent quality of life, and ending their suffering should be okay. It does not mean we don't want to save all healthy, safe animals. I firmly believe in and support the no-kill movement.*

I started writing again a few weeks ago for the first time in two years. I began a new blog and have published a couple of articles. Those were both lead-ins to this story I knew I needed to write, but which I have been avoiding.

Some of you may have noticed when my blog went silent and I no longer posted articles and opinion pieces on social media. I didn't stop writing gradually. I stopped suddenly and completely on December 3, 2017. That was the day that Bosco attacked me and changed my world forever. Until now I have never written about (or even really spoken about) that night. It was too life-changing, too violent, too painful and too traumatizing to even begin to wrap my head around, let alone make sense of it all for the outside world.

In part there is some undeserved shame involved. Kevin and I were (and are) extremely vocal pit bull type dog advocates, and now I had been injured by just that kind of dog. The anti-pit crowd had a field day with the event. In their minds it validated everything they had been saying about what they called monster dogs. In truth, it validated what we, and the rest of the rescue world, had been saying: that each dog is an individual. A product of breeding, training, socialization, and experiences. And in Bosco's case, in all probability, physical health and well-being. Bosco didn't attack me because of his breed. He attacked me because something was haywire in this brain.

When we look back at videos of Bosco it is extremely apparet that he was in a steep downward spiral behavior-wise. Day by day, week by week, his behavior deteriorated. This was not an emotionally or mentally healthy dog and strange things tended to set him off unexpectedly. His biggest bugaboo was "stranger danger" and we could not safely have any other person in our home, including family members.

The day that we were expecting a visit from the internet service tech, Kevin and I took turns driving him around for hours. And when he got home and realized someone had been in the house, he was frantic and reactive.

Although Bosco always had questionable people skills, he had amazing dog skills. And that's when we really noticed we had an issue; when his dog skills started deteriorating rapidly.

One evening he and Turtle got into a scrap and it quickly escalated into something that could have ended badly for Turtle. She has no teeth to protect herself, but she the tenacity of her former fighting life to keep her from backing down. Kevin got his hand in the middle and took a pretty bad bite. He was out of commission so I jumped in to try and shut things down by grabbing the citronella spray and shooting it into the the snarling knot of dogs, which successfully drove them apart. Without even taking a beat Bosco launched himself at me. I threw my arm up in front of my face and he latched on, biting me badly. He was gathering himself to spring again and would have if I hadn't sprayed him in the face with the citronella. He scared me to death that night because there was no one home in his eyes when he went for me. No recognition, no expression...just flat shark-like eyes.

The next day I was seeking advice from people I worked with at the sanctuary, including my supervisor and behavioral specialists. I was really looking for someone to validate what I was thinking; that this dog was not safe and should be humanely euthanized. Against my better judgement I allowed people to convince me that I needed to try and work with Bosco. I am not blaming any of them for their advice. I was the only one who had seen his attack and I knew he was not safe. But I didn't want to make the hard decision. I grabbed hold of the suggestions with all my might, to try and "fix" Bosco's issues.

I was directed to try nutritional supplements, increased exercise via a treadmill instead of walks, as they were too triggering. And finally we decided to explore drug therapy to try and get Bosco back on the right track.

Then the night of December 3rd came. It was quiet time for the dogs so that our birds could come out of their cages and socialize. That meant the dogs retired to separate rooms and crates. Each one got a kong or a marrow bone to keep them occupied. Bosco could be very crate aggressive, so we kept the door to the crate in the living room closed so he didn't feel the need to protect it. That wasn't even his crate, but that really didn't matter to him. I was just luring Bosco into his room with a treat when Turtle nudged open the living room crate in happy anticipation of getting her evening bone. Bosco lunged past me and went for Turtle. I raced to try and hold the door of the crate closed with my leg. Bosco decided that if he couldn't get at Turtle, I would do just fine, so he redirected on me.

Bosco took me down to the floor before I could even realize what was happening, severing a finger on my left hand and totally shattering all the bones in my right arm from wrist to elbow. If Kevin hadn't grabbed a can of bear spray that had been a gift from Vicktory Dog Lance's people, I would never have survived that night.

Bosco had to be killed that night while I was being ambulanced to the hospital an hour and a half away. He didn't have the dignity of a calm and supported, peaceful euthanization. Instead he endured the trauma of his own emotions and behaviors, and died in a state of
reactivity and violence. He deserved better.

I am eternally thankful that Bosco attacked me and not someone else. I could not have lived with myself if he had gotten loose and attacked a child or even an adult. I found out very graphically how quickly a human can be incapacitated by an attacking dog. I wouldn't wish that one anyone, ever.

Bosco should have been humanely euthanized the first time he bit me. There should have been no question. If he could react that way to someone he lived with and cared for, he was not a safe dog to have in a home. I should not have allowed myself to be talked out of taking the steps I knew to be necessary. And there is one other consideration. If I had made the decision to euthanize him for behavior I would have had a fight on my hands from our clinic and maybe from his rescue organization as well. People might have tried to talk me into relinquishing him to rescue. When Bosco was good he seemed like a goofy, silly little clown of a dog. What if people didn't look past that and he had been adopted out again?

Yes, we want to save dogs who are healthy and adoptable. No dog should ever be killed who could thrive in a home. But in some ways, I believe it is immoral to try and save dogs who cannot have a decent quality of life, regardless if it's because of a debilitating physical issue or a mental one.

A dog who is not safe around humans should never be adopted into a home, and we need to stop stigmatizing people who make the call to euthanize their dogs for an issue they recognize. If Bosco had been suffering from a painful disease that was untreatable, no one would have an issue with helping him cross. The same should hold true for a dog who is suffering from a mental condition that causes his life to be unhappy or full of mental pain.

There are many, many happy healthy dogs we should concentrate on saving. But we need to be realistic about dogs who may not be safe to save. There are finite resources out there; let's utilize them saving the dogs we can. We cannot, nor should we try, to save each and every one.

ABOUT THE AUTHOR

Jacqueline C. Johnson

Jacqueline and her husband Kevin spent 10 years living and working at the country's largest no-kill sanctuary. While there they had the good fortune to meet and work with many of the dogs rescued from Michael Vick's Bad Newz Kennels. Today the Johnson's are back in their native South Dakota, living with 3 adopted pit bull terrier type dogs and enjoying their children and grandchildren.

Made in the USA
Middletown, DE
25 November 2020